You Might Be
A Redneck If...

– ◆ –

JEFF FOXWORTHY

– ◆ –

Illustrations by David Boyd

LONGSTREET PRESS
Atlanta, Georgia

Published by
LONGSTREET PRESS, INC.
A subsidiary of Cox Newspapers,
A subsidiary of Cox Enterprises, Inc.
2140 Newmarket Parkway
Suite 118
Marietta, GA 30067

Printed in the United States of America

21th printing, 1994

Library of Congress Catalog Number 89-080277

ISBN 0-929264-57-6

This book was printed by Data Reproductions Corporation, Rochester Hills, Michigan. The text was set in ITC Clearface Regular by Typo-Repro Service, Inc., Atlanta, Georgia. Cover illustration by David Boyd. Cover design by David Levy, Atlanta, Georgia.
Part of the *YOU MIGHT BE A REDNECK IF* . . . series by Jeff Foxworthy

Foreword

I had the pleasure to host Jeff Foxworthy on my HBO special, "Opening Night at Rodney's Place," this summer. He was great!

Being a comedian, I can really appreciate the cleverness of Jeff's material and his super execution of it.

Jeff also has humility as a person, which comes through when you watch him perform. That's a great asset, whether you're in show business or not.

Jeff's observations on being a redneck are really funny. I'm not trying to compete with him in that area, but they impressed me so much that I thought of a couple myself. Here goes:

— You might be a redneck if you swear you're not drunk and then pass out.

— You might be a redneck if you need someone to help you read this book.

So here's to Jeff Foxworthy and his great future. He can make me laugh anytime.

Rodney Dangerfield

ACKNOWLEDGEMENTS

With heartfelt thanks to Gregg, Chris DiPetta, Lisa Bartlett, Vic Henley, Ron White, Mike Venneman, Tim Wilson, Vicki Grethe and Elliott Vincent for their contributions to this noble project.

DEDICATION

For my extraordinary wife, without whose love and support my life would run like a monster truck with a bad transmission.

Introduction

Long before the first cat hat was donned, the first cherry-bomb muffler installed, or the first pop-top bracelet created, Rednecks roamed the earth.

Nobody knows exactly where they came from or who the first one was. Maybe they descended from a caveman who liked to scratch a lot while admiring the prehistoric kill of the day, or maybe from a Roman soldier who put taps on his sandals and fuzzy dice on his chariot. Regardless of their roots, today they not only survive, they flourish.

A common misconception is that Rednecks are confined to warmer climates and speak with a Southern accent, but nothing could be further from the truth. Rednecks are very durable characters and can adapt to any climate (with the help of flannel and chenille). My profession takes me all over this country, and I've seen Rednecks in every corner of every state.

For example, there is a bowling alley in Michigan that has valet parking for its customers. That's almost a baited field for Rednecks out on the town. And what about those beer-swilling crazies in the bleachers of New York's Shea Stadium? We're talking bright red. And California beach bums are nothing more than laid-back Rednecks dressed in funny clothes.

I suspect that most of us have a little Redneck flowing through our veins. I know I do. Some of our national heroes—like Babe Ruth and Elvis Presley—also were a little pink around the collar, and we loved them for it.

My point is that Redneck is not a term of derision; it's a state of mind. And therefore it is with pride that I reach deep into the cooler, pull out a cold one, and toast everyone who has ever visited (or lived in) that state.

—J.F.

You might be a redneck if...

Your richest relative buys a new house
and you have to help take
the wheels off of it.

– ✧ –

You've ever used lard in bed.

– ✧ –

You think potted meat on a saltine
is an hors d'oeuvre.

You might be a redneck if...

You own more than three shirts with
the sleeves cut off.

– ✧ –

You've ever spraypainted your
girlfriend's name on an overpass.

– ✧ –

You've ever been blacklisted
from a bowling alley.

You might be a redneck if...

Your high school annual is now a mug shot book for the police department.

You might be a redneck if...

The highlight of your family reunion
was your sister's nude dancing debut.

– ✧ –

You've ever done your Christmas
shopping at a truck stop.

– ✧ –

You think heaven looks a lot like
Daytona Beach, Florida.

You might be a redneck if...

There is a stuffed 'possum mounted
anywhere in your home.

You might be a redneck if...

You consider a six pack of beer and a
bug-zapper quality entertainment.

You might be a redneck if...

Your lifetime goal is to own your own fireworks stand.

– ✧ –

You prefer to walk the excess length off your jeans rather than hem them.

– ✧ –

You go to a stock car race and don't need a program.

You might be a redneck if...

Someone asks to see your I.D. and
you show them your belt buckle.

You might be a redneck if...

Your junior-senior prom had
a day-care center.

– ✧ –

Less than half the cars you own run.

– ✧ –

You grow your sideburns longer and
fuller because it looks so
good on your sister.

You might be a redneck if...

Your mother does not remove the
Marlboro from her lips before telling
the state patrolman to kiss her ass.

You might be a redneck if....

The primary color of your car
is "Bond-O."

– ◇ –

Your mounted deer head sports
a baseball cap and sunglasses.

– ◇ –

You have Pabst Blue Ribbon
on tap in your bathroom.

You might be a redneck if...

Your pocketknife often doubles as a toothpick.

You might be a redneck if...

You are having marital problems
because your wife never lets
you win at arm wrestling.

– ◈ –

You own a denim leisure suit.

– ◈ –

Directions to your house include
"turn off the paved road."

You might be a redneck if...

The U.F.O. Hotline limits you to one call per day.

You might be a redneck if...

You know how many bales of hay
your car can hold.

– ✧ –

You've ever used a Weed Eater indoors.

– ✧ –

You honest-to-God think women are
turned on by animal noises and
seductive tongue gestures.

You might be a redneck if...

Your dog and your wallet are both on a chain.

You might be a redneck if...

The kids are going hungry tonight
because you just had to have the
Yosemite Sam mud flaps.

Your dog has a litter of puppies on the
living room floor and nobody notices.

You've ever been kicked out of the
KKK for being a "bigot."

17

You might be a redneck if...

You made a homemade hot-tub with a trolling motor.

You might be a redneck if...

You use your mailbox to hold up one
end of your clothesline.

You might be a redneck if…

You don't think baseball players
spit and scratch too much.

— ✧ —

You owe a taxidermist more than
your annual income.

— ✧ —

During your wedding, when you kissed
the bride, your John Deere hat fell off.

You might be a redneck if...

You've ever lost
a tooth opening
a beer bottle.

You might be a redneck if...

Hail hits your house and you
have to take it to the body shop
for an estimate.

– ✧ –

You use a bedsheet as a sofa cover.

– ✧ –

Jack Daniels makes your list of
most admired people.

You might be a redneck if...

You have a tattoo that says "Mother"
and it's spelled wrong.

You might be a redneck if...

You didn't put the pink plastic
flamingoes in your front yard as a joke.

The manager of the sewage
treatment plant tells you it's time
to wash your hair.

Everybody you meet can tell what kind
of underwear you're wearing.

You might be a redneck if...

Your family tree
does not fork.

You might be a redneck if…

Your wife's hairdo has ever been
ruined by a ceiling fan.

You might be a redneck if...

You see no need to stop at rest stops
because you have an empty milk jug
in the car.

You had a toothpick in your mouth
when your wedding pictures
were taken.

You have a rag for a gas cap.

You might be a redneck if...

You think God looks a lot like Hank Williams, Jr.

You might be a redneck if...

A man lights your cigarette and
you show him your bra.

The dog can't watch you eat
without gagging.

The crack in your windshield is longer
than your arm . . . and has been for
more than a year.

You might be a redneck if...

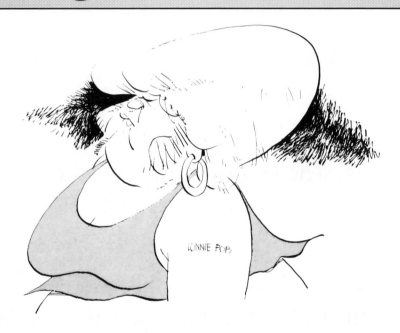

You show your boyfriend you really love him
by carving his name on your arm.

You might be a redneck if...

You have to dress up the kids
to go to K-Mart.

– ✧ –

You have a Hefty Bag for a
passenger-side window.

– ✧ –

You've ever hollered, "Rock the house,
Bubba!" during a piano recital.

You might be a redneck if...

Thanksgiving dinner was ruined because you ran out of ketchup.

You might be a redneck if...

Your mother has ever been involved in a
fistfight at a high school sports event.

You might be a redneck if...

Your watchband is wider than any
book you've ever read.

You've ever had to turn your pick-up
truck around because of bridge
clearance restrictions.

You've ever barbequed Spam
on the grill.

You might be a redneck if...

You are famous for your homemade squash wine.

You might be a redneck if...

You've ever had to scratch your sister's
name out of a message that begins,
"For a good time call . . . ."

You have to recrank your car
at every intersection.

The neighbors started a petition over
your Christmas lights.

You might be a redneck if...

You've ever ridden all the way to
Florida with your bare feet
hanging out the car window.

You might be a redneck if…

You ever "hit on" somebody
in a V.D. clinic.

– ✧ –

You view duct tape as
a long-term investment.

– ✧ –

You regularly answer the question
"What have you been doing lately?"
with "Partying."

You might be a redneck if...

Your grandmother has ever stopped to relieve herself on the side of the highway.

You might be a redneck if...

Your brother-in-law is also your uncle.

– ✧ –

You grow corn in your front yard.

– ✧ –

You have refused to watch the
Academy Awards since *Smokey and
the Bandit* was snubbed
for best picture.

You might be a redneck if...

You've ever hit a bump on the highway and
lost half of your worldly possessions.

You might be a redneck if...

You bought a VCR because wrestling is
on while you're at work.

$-$ ✧ $-$

Red Man Chewing Tobacco sends you
a Christmas card.

$-$ ✧ $-$

Every workday ends with the same
argument about who gets to ride in
the cab of the truck.

You might be a redneck if...

You've ever hit
a jukebox with
a cue stick.

You might be a redneck if...

Your dad walks you to school because
you're in the same grade.

– ✧ –

You've ever stolen a bulldozer.

– ✧ –

After the prom you drove the truck
while your date hit road signs
with beer bottles.

You might be a redneck if...

Your father fully executes the "pull my finger" trick during Christmas dinner.

You might be a redneck if...

The rear tires on your car are
twice as wide as the front ones.

– ✧ –

All of your four-letter words
are two syllables.

– ✧ –

You cut your toenails
in front of company.

You might be a redneck if...

You've ever been too drunk to fish.

You might be a redneck if...

You view the upcoming family reunion
as a chance to meet women.

– ✧ –

Hitchhikers won't get in the
car with you.

– ✧ –

Your wife has a beer belly and
you find it attractive.

You might be a redneck if...

FIRST TEAM ALL AMERICAN CHITTLIN' EATER

RECORD CARP CATCH CHATAHOOCHIE RIVER 1981

1ST PLACE CHUG·A·LUG CONTEST

You prominently display a gift you
bought at Graceland.

You might be a redneck if...

You've ever heard a sheep bleat and
had romantic thoughts.

Your house doesn't have curtains
but your truck does.

No matter which side of the track
you live on, it's the wrong side.

You might be a redneck if...

Your front porch collapses and
kills more than three dogs.

You might be a redneck if...

The front license plate of your car
has the words "Foxy Lady"
written in airbrush.

You wonder how service stations keep
their restrooms so clean.

You think "The dishwasher is broke"
means your wife has no money.

You might be a redneck if...

You can spit
without opening
your mouth.

You might be a redneck if...

You buy a color-coordinated rope to tie down your car hood.

You've ever started a petition to have the National Anthem changed to "Freebird."

You consider *Outdoor Life* deep reading.

You might be a redneck if...

You've ever written Richard Petty's name on a presidential ballot.

You might be a redneck if...

The "Save Naugahyde" protection
group chooses your house
as a picket site.

– ◇ –

You call your boss "dude."

– ◇ –

Your new job promotion means the
company foots the bill to have your
name sewn on your shirts.

You think a
Volvo is part of
a woman's anatomy.

You might be a redneck if...

The diploma hanging in your
den includes the words
"Trucking Institute."

– ✧ –

You have grease under your toenails.

– ✧ –

You consider your license plate "personalized"
because your father made it.

You might be a redneck if...

Your mother keeps a spit cup on
the ironing board.

You might be a redneck if...

You think Dom Perignon is
a Mafia leader.

– –

The most common phrase you
hear at your family reunion is
"What the hell are you
lookin' at, Diphead?"

– ◇ –

You honest-to-God in your heart
believe that Ted Nugent rules.

You might be a redneck if...

You've ever driven
a Camaro into
the top of a tree.

You might be a redneck if...

You've ever been fired from
a construction job due
to your appearance.

– ◇ –

The fountain at your wedding spewed beer
instead of champagne.

– ◇ –

You think beef jerky and Moon Pies
are two of the major food groups.

You might be a redneck if...

You've ever worn a tube top to a wedding.

You might be a redneck if...

You are allowed to bring
your dog to work.

– ✧ –

You've ever cleaned fish
in your living room.

– ✧ –

You've ever had to haul a can of paint
to the top of a water tower to defend
your sister's honor.

You might be a redneck if...

A man asks you to dance and you take
off your clothes and climb on a table.

You might be a redneck if...

You think Campho-Phenique is
a miracle drug.

You have more than two brothers
named Bubba or Junior.

During your wedding ceremony the
minister said, "Do you, DeWayne, take
Connie to be your old lady?"

You might be a redneck if...

You think the Styrofoam cooler is the
greatest invention of all time.

You might be a redneck if...

You actually know which kind of
leaves make the best substitute
for toilet paper.

There is a laminated picture of Rambo
on your headboard.

After removing the empty beer cans from
your car you find you get
fifteen more miles to the gallon.

You might be a redneck if...

Your mother genuinely admires your girlfriend's tattoos.

You might be a redneck if...

You pawned your grandfather's pocket watch because you needed beer money for the weekend.

It's impossible to see food stains on the fabric of your work uniform.

You need one more hole punched in your card before you get a "freebie" at the House of Tattoos.

70

You might be a redneck if...

You've ever had sex in a satellite dish.

You might be a redneck if...

Your father encourages you to quit
school because Larry has an
opening on the lube rack.

– –

You wore a three-day growth of
beard before Don Johnson.

– ✧ –

Someone asks to see your marriage
license and you have to dig through
the back floorboard of the G.T.O.

You might be a redneck if...

You get an estimate from the barber
before he cuts your hair.

You might be a redneck if...

Your sister's educational goal is
to get out of high school
before she gets pregnant.

– ◇ –

After making love you have to ask your
date to roll down the window.

– ◇ –

You wear knee-high stockings
with a skirt.